GLACIERS

GLACIERS

ROY A. GALLANT

A FIRST BOOK

Franklin Watts
A Division of Scholastic Inc.
New York Toronto London Auckland Sydney
Mexico City New Delhi Hong Kong
Danbury, Connecticut

For Jeannine

Photographs ©: Bob & Ira Spring: chapter openers, cover, 18; Bob Clemenz Photography: 36 bottom, 42, 43; NASA: 12; Peter Arnold Inc.: 6 (S.J. Krasemann); Photo Researchers: 17 (William W. Bacon), 11 (Tim Davis), 10, 48 (Simon Fraser/SPL), 22 (David Vaughan/SPL), 26 (Charles D. Winters); Reuters/Archive Photos: 35 (Arni Saeberg-Morgunblid); The Ohio State University Archives: 46, 47; Tony Stone Images: 8 (James Balog), 30 (Brett Baunton), 24, 25 (Tom Bean), 21 (Ed Collacott), 28 (Daniel J. Cox), 36 top (David Hiser), 50 (Rhonda Klevansky), 14 (World Prospective), 2 (Olaf Soot), 52, 53 (John Turner), 38, 39, 40 (Paul Wakefield), 16; UPI/Corbis-Bettmann: 27; Visuals Unlimited: 33 (John D. Cunningham).

Library of Congress Cataloging-in-Publication Data

Gallant, Roy A.
     Glaciers / by Roy A. Gallant
     (A First book)
     Includes biographical references and index.
     Summary: Discusses the formation and movement of glaciers, how they reflect the history of Earth, and how they affect life around them.
          ISBN 0-531-20390-5 (lib. bdg.)   0-531-15956-6 (pbk.)
          1. Glaciers—Juvenile literature. 2. Glaciers—United States—Juvenile literature.[1. Glaciers.] I. Title. II. Series.
GB2403.8.G347   1999
551.31'2—dc21   98-4162
                                                                         CIP
                                                                         AC

CONTENTS

In many parts of North America, thin layers of ice form on top of puddles and small ponds in late fall.

When Ice Doesn't Melt

As fall turns to winter, the air temperature sometimes drops below freezing during the night. When people wake up in the morning, a thin skin of ice glazes the surfaces of small ponds. But by noon, the ice is gone.

Over the next few weeks, the air grows colder. Soon, the sun's rays don't give off enough heat to melt the ice. Each night the water in the pond loses more of its summer heat, and the layer of ice on the pond grows thicker. As the water freezes, you may be able to hear it groaning, creaking, or ringing.

When the first snow falls, it sticks to the ice. Soon layers of ice form on top of the snow. As winter continues, layer after layer of ice is laid down on the pond. But when warmer spring temperatures return, all the ice and snow melt away. This is what happens every year in most parts of North America.

Mount McKinley in Alaska is covered with snow all year long.

But just imagine what would happen if the ice and snow never disappeared. What if the air temperature did not warm up enough to melt the ice that covers ponds, lakes, and even the land each winter? This is exactly what happens in the parts of the world surrounding the North Pole and the South Pole.

Where Ice Rules

In the northernmost regions of Canada, Alaska, Europe, Greenland, and Russia, the snow never melts. In the Southern Hemisphere, Antarctica is a solid sheet of ice all year long. And in many other parts of the world, the snow that falls on the tallest mountains never disappears completely. It continues to pile up month after month, year after year, century after century. Eventually, enough snow builds up to form huge *glaciers*.

The world's greatest glaciers are found near the poles and on top of high mountains because these are the coldest places on Earth. The polar regions are cold because they get less sunlight than other parts of the world. In fact, in the middle of winter, the land above the Arctic Circle is in total darkness for several weeks.

Since our planet is tilted on an *axis*, the North Pole points away from the sun when it is winter in the Northern Hemisphere. As a result, areas in the northern half of the world have long nights and short days. Meanwhile, in Antarctica, it is summer, and the sun is shining all day

The midnight sun over Greenland

and all night. Six months later, the Southern Hemisphere will be in the darkness of winter and the sun will be shining at midnight in parts of Alaska, Greenland, and Russia.

Even though polar regions are so sunny in summer, the temperature rarely rises above freezing, and very little of the snow melts. Because Earth is round, the light that shines on the polar regions hits the planet at a sharp angle. On its way to the ground, the sunlight passes through a lot more *atmosphere* than the sunlight that

Although the African country of Kenya is hot all year long, the snow on top of Mt. Kilimanjaro never melts.

shines on land near the equator. All that extra atmosphere absorbs some of the heat of the sun's rays. So, by the time the sunlight reaches the ground, there isn't much heat left to warm the land and melt the snow.

Because tall mountains rise up into the atmosphere, you might think they would be warmed more quickly than the land below. This doesn't happen, however, because the atmosphere is thin and cools rapidly at night. Even though the atmosphere absorbs large amounts of heat from the sun, it is always much colder than the land below it. That's why very tall mountains are covered with snow all year long.

Snowy areas, including the Antarctic ice sheet, are visible in this picture of Earth taken from space.

2

What Is a Glacier?

Have you ever seen a photograph of Earth from space? To astronauts onboard the Space Shuttle, our planet looks blue, brown, and white. The blue area is the oceans, and the brown area is the land. Most of the white area is clouds, but some of it is ice.

Today, ice covers about 10 percent of our planet. More than 95 percent of that ice covers Antarctica and Greenland as giant ice sheets, but every continent except Australia has some glaciers all year round. A glacier is a large body of ice and snow that moves outward or downhill under its own weight. Glaciers are made up of snow and ice that has built up over many years. If only a little more snow falls during the winter than melts during the summer, it may take 100 years for a glacier to form. But in areas where snowfall is heavy, a glacier may form in as little as 10 years.

A view of the southern tip of Greenland from space

Two Kinds of Glaciers

There are two main types of glaciers—*ice sheets* and *valley glaciers*. Ice sheets are enormous, thick mounds of ice that cover large areas of land surrounding the North Pole and the South Pole. The tremendous weight of an ice sheet causes it to spread outward in all directions. An ice sheet is so thick that it hides almost all the features of the land below it, and some ice sheets are large enough to cover an entire continent.

Today, there are two major ice sheets in the world. One covers Antarctica, and the other covers Greenland. These huge ice sheets are also called ice caps. Near the South Pole, the Antarctic ice sheet is more than 2 miles (3 km) thick. Scientists think that this ice sheet has existed for at least 10 million years. Greenland's ice sheet is not quite as thick, but if it were spread evenly over the surface of the world, it would be 17 feet (5 m) thick. That's a lot of ice! Smaller ice sheets are found in western Europe, Iceland, and northeastern Canada. Large areas of the Arctic Ocean are also covered by an ice sheet.

Valley glaciers are like solid rivers of ice. They "flow" down the valleys between very tall mountains. Most form when the tremendous weight of snow piled at the top of a mountain causes avalanches to tumble down steep mountain slopes. The snow then forms a giant block of ice and begins to move slowly downward under the force of *gravity*. This type of glacier cannot spread

Tasman Glacier in South Canterbury, New Zealand is a valley glacier.

outward because it is confined by the mountains surrounding it. But when a valley glacier reaches a large, flat plain, it spreads out in all directions. At this point, it is called a *piedmont glacier*.

Valley glaciers are found all over the world. In the United States, you can visit valley glaciers in California, Oregon, Washington, Montana, Colorado, and Wyoming. In Europe, valley glaciers are scattered throughout the Alps, the Pyrenees, and the Caucasus Mountains. In Asia,

Hubbard Glacier in Alaska is one of the largest glaciers in the world.

the Himalaya, the Hindu Kush, the Karakoram, and the Kunlun ranges have valley glaciers. The Andes mountains in South America, the Southern Alps in New Zealand, and Mount Kilimanjaro in Africa also have valley glaciers.

Most are only a few hundred feet long, but some are huge. The world's largest valley glaciers include Lambert Glacier in Antarctica, which is more than 200 miles (320 km) long, and Hubbard Glacier in Alaska, which is 75 miles (120 km) long.

17

A park ranger leads a group of hikers past a crevasse in Grinnell Glacier in Glacier National Park, Montana.

GLACIERS ON THE MOVE

In 1933, two park rangers were hiking across Lyell Glacier in Yosemite National Park in California. It was a warm, sunny day, and the rangers were enjoying the view. As they looked around, one of the rangers was startled by what he saw—a mountain sheep staring right at him. The ranger knew this wasn't just any sheep—the animal he was looking at was supposed to be *extinct*.

As the rangers moved slowly toward the sheep, they were amazed that it didn't run away. It stood as still as a statue. When the rangers touched the animal, they knew why it hadn't moved—it was frozen solid. The sheep had died a long, long time ago, but had been perfectly preserved by the ice. Because it had a broken neck, scientists concluded that the animal died when it fell into a huge *crevasse*—a crack—in the glacier. The sheep had been buried below tons of ice for many years, but as the glacier slowly moved and melted at the end, its body was uncovered. The rangers who discovered the mountain sheep just happened to be in the right place at the right time.

How a Glacier Forms

Glaciers are made up of snow and ice that has accumulated over many years, but not every permanent pile of snow and ice is a glacier. A mound of snow and ice can be called a glacier only if it moves under its own weight.

When fresh snow falls on top of last year's snow, its weight presses the snowflakes underneath together to form a coarse, grainy material called *firn*. Year after year, more layers of snow fall on top of the firn. More snow means more weight and more pressure. The crystals deep within the snow pile are crushed and compacted by the weight of the layers on top of them.

Eventually, the lower layers become much denser than layers close to the surface. Finally, the snow particles can't take any more pressure, so they melt and then refreeze to form ice. At the same time, meltwater from the top of the giant snowpile seeps down into the firn. When that water refreezes, it too forms ice.

By the time a permanent snowpile is about 200 feet (60 m) high, the tremendous pressure within the pile has turned the bottom layers to solid ice. Although that ice is solid, it is not hard or brittle. In fact, it is more like

This glacier has moved down a mountain and spread out over a flat area.

toothpaste than the ice that you have probably seen coating trees or sidewalks in the winter.

As you know, if a tube of toothpaste is capped, it is easy to move the toothpaste back and forth inside the tube. Similarly, the ice at the bottom of the snowpile begins to spread out or flow downhill. Once the snowpile starts to move, it is called a glacier. A thin film of water at the bottom of the glacier helps the huge mass of ice and snow slide over the land.

Galloping Glaciers

As a glacier moves, not all of it travels at the same speed. The soft pressurized ice near the bottom of the glacier moves more quickly than the ice and snow above it. As a result, the brittle ice in the center of the glacier often cracks and shatters to form crevasses.

A scientist on a glacier in Antarctica is measuring his position to calculate the glacier's speed.

To study a glacier's movement, scientists drill holes in the ice and then stick a stake into each hole. By keeping track of the positions of the stakes over weeks and months, the researchers can calculate how quickly and in what direction a glacier is moving.

An average valley glacier flows down a mountain at about 650 feet (200 m) a year, but a few move about 3 miles (5 km) in just 1 year. Sometimes glaciers move in irregular spurts. These "galloping glaciers" may travel 4 miles (6 km) in only a few months and then slow down. One of the fastest glaciers on record is the Kutiah Valley Glacier in India. In 1953, it flowed farther than the length of a football field every day for 3 months.

What Is an Iceberg?

When a glacier reaches the edge of the land, it usually flows into the ocean. Because ice is less dense than water, the glacier is lifted up as it begins to float on the water's surface. In many cases, this lifting causes the glacier to snap at its weakest points—usually along crevasses. The smaller chunks—known as *icebergs*—fall into the ocean with a thundering sound that echoes for miles. This process is called *calving*.

Between 10,000 and 15,000 icebergs calve off the Greenland ice cap each year. Many are caught up in ocean currents and carried to busy shipping lanes.

A calving glacier

Why Icebergs Don't Sink

Every material can exist in three different forms—a solid, a liquid, and a gas. In most substances, the solid form is more dense than the liquid form. Density is the measurement that tells us how light or heavy something is compared to its size. This means that if you have the same volume of water (a liquid) and ice (a solid), you might expect the ice to weigh more.

If this were true, when you put an ice cube in a glass of water, it would sink. But this is not what happens. Ice floats in water. Water does not follow the same rules as most materials.

Ice moves to the top of a glass of water.

**The _Titanic_ before it hit an iceberg on its journey
to the United States.**

In 1912, the "unsinkable" _Titanic_ struck an iceberg in
the North Atlantic. The ice tore a 300-foot (91-m) gash
in the ship's hull. Within 3 hours, the _Titanic_ went down.
Because the ship did not have enough lifeboats for all its
passengers, more than 1,500 people died in the icy wa-
ters before help arrived.

No two icebergs are exactly alike. They come in
many shapes and sizes. Icebergs are often as large as

This iceberg looks pretty big, but the portion below
the water is much, much larger.

5,000 feet (1,500 m) long and as tall as a 30-story building. In 1956, a United States Navy icebreaker reported an Antarctic iceberg that measured 60 miles (97 km) wide and 208 miles (335 km) long. That's larger than the state of Massachusetts!

There are plenty of icebergs in the oceans surrounding Antarctica, too. In 1996, scientists noticed an iceberg about the same size as the state of Rhode Island. Experts predict that it will take at least 10 years for this iceberg to melt.

If you see a photograph of an iceberg, it might not seem that large to you, but looks can be deceiving. Many sailors have learned the hard way that most of an iceberg lies underwater. In fact, the part of the iceberg below the ocean's surface is usually eight or nine times larger than the part we see above the water.

Today only about 10 percent of Earth is covered with glaciers like this one in Mt. Baker Wilderness Area, Washington. In the last 1 million years, however, glaciers have periodically spread over large portions of the planet.

GLACIERS OF THE PAST

Today, only the top and bottom of our planet—the poles—are capped with thick blankets of ice. But at certain times in Earth's history, as much as 30 percent of the planet was covered with ice. At other times, Earth had little or no permanent ice. In fact, for more than 90 percent of the past 570 million years, the polar regions have probably been completely free of ice.

During the last 1 million years, however, Earth has been relatively cold. Scientists believe that glacial ice may have advanced and retreated as many as nine times. So, although there is very little ice on Earth today, there will most likely come a time when the ice advances again. If it does, a great wall of moving ice may scrape New York, Montreal, and Chicago off the map. The ruins of these great cities may be pushed southward and heaped up on top of Tampa, St. Louis, or New Orleans.

Before glaciers can crawl over large areas the world, a huge quantity of ocean water must evaporate into the atmosphere and air temperatures all over the world must fall. If this happens, more water than normal returns to the ground as snow. It will snow and snow and snow. When summer comes, only some of the snow will melt. And because the moisture given up by the oceans will not be replaced by spring meltwaters, sea level will begin to fall. During the last *ice age*, sea level may have fallen as much as 360 feet (110 m).

Year after year, the snow will continue to build up. The firn deep within the snowpiles will be squished and squeezed by the weight of the snow above it. Eventually, the firn will melt and glaciers will form. As long as the air temperature stays low, the glaciers will slowly spread outward and slide downward. Each year, more and more of Earth will be covered with ice.

An Icy Earth

A typical ice age, or glacial period, lasts about 100,000 years. Between two glacial periods there is a warmer time called an *interglacial period*. Most interglacial periods last about 10,000 years.

The most recent glacial period peaked about 18,000 years ago. At that time, ice covered large areas of land and oceans in both the Northern and Southern Hemispheres. The ice was about 5,000 feet (1,500 m) thick in

During the most recent ice age, food was scarce. Humans and predators such as saber-toothed tigers competed for mammoths and other large mammals.

what is now New England and 2 miles (3.2 km) thick in what is now eastern Canada.

For a glacial period to end, temperatures all over the planet must begin to rise. When this happens, the great ice sheets and valley glaciers gradually melt and sea level begins to rise. Coastal areas all over the world are flooded, and the edges of the continents are given new shapes. Inland flooding is also common.

When an ancient lake in western Montana over-flowed a dam created by a glacier, the rampaging water sped westward. It scooped up the floors of many small valleys and turned them into deep trenches. We can still see the results of that destruction. One example is the Grand Coulee, a giant, steep-walled hole in Washington state.

In some parts of the world, floods caused by glacial meltwaters still occur. The island country of Iceland lies just below the Arctic Circle. It is sometimes called "the land of fire and ice" because ice sheets there lie next to— and even on top of—active volcanoes and hot springs.

From time to time, a volcano below a glacier erupts. The molten rock that spews out of the volcano melts the ice above it. As the ice melts, it forms a pool of water about 1,000 feet (305 m) deep. When the water finally melts through the ice damming it, the force of gravity pulls the water down the valley and the land is flooded. As this *jökulhlaup* rushes through villages and over the countryside at up to 60 miles (100 km) an

On October 4, 1996, a volcano erupted beneath Vatnajokull Glacier in Iceland. The eruption broke through the glacial ice and spewed ash 15,000 feet (4,500 m) into the air.

From this photo (left), it is easy to imagine the path that glacial ice once took as it flowed down between the mountains. At one time, glacial ice covered this mountain (below). The tremendous weight of the ice caused part of the mountain to collapse, creating a horseshoe shape.

hour, it sweeps away everything in its path—huge boulders and trees, cars and buildings, and even people. These horrible floods occur every other year, with an especially bad one every 5 years. The most recent jökulhlaup, the worst of the century, devastated Iceland in 1996.

How Glaciers Sculpt the Land

Glaciologists—scientists who study glaciers—know that glaciers have advanced and retreated many times during Earth's history because they can see how the ice has shaped and reshaped the land. As a glacier slides across Earth's surface, it cuts and grinds the uppermost layers of rock and soil, and then carries away the loosened material. It deepens river valleys by scooping up the valley floors, and widens them by scraping away the walls.

Meanwhile, the tremendous weight of the glacier often causes the land beneath it to sink. Areas of land just north of the Great Lakes sank as much as 1,000 feet (305 m) during the most recent ice age. Now that the land is free of ice, it is slowly rising again. Large areas of land in Sweden, Norway, and Finland are also slowly rebounding from the great weight of that ancient ice.

All the debris dug up by a gliding glacier is dragged along for miles and then dumped in one spot. This deposited material is known as a *moraine*. Some moraines

This moraine was deposited by a glacier that flowed across Iceland thousands of years ago.

are quite large. Cape Cod, the peninsula on the eastern end of Massachusetts, and Long Island, off the coast of New York, are both moraines. They were formed when ancient mountains of moving ice bulldozed and then dumped tons and tons of rock and soil.

A moraine is a telltale sign that a glacier once passed over an area. But there are other clues, too. Streams that ran through tunnels in melting glaciers sometimes

deposited very long, steep-sided mounds of sand and gravel that twist and turn across the land. On average, these mounds are about 30 feet (9 m) high and 30 feet (9 m) wide.

When giant blocks of ice broke off glaciers, gravel and sand often built up new land around the ice block. When the ice melted, huge bowl-shaped pits, called kettles, were left behind. These kettles are generally about

The rocks scattered over this field in Ireland were left behind by an ancient glacier.

100 feet (30 m) deep and at least 1 mile (1.6 km) across, but they may be larger or smaller.

Look for groups of massive boulders in the middle of the woods or in a field. If they are different from other nearby rocks, they may have been left behind by a glacier.

In central Minnesota and New England, glaciers often deposited massive piles of sand and gravel. On average, the tear-shaped hills that formed are about 100 feet (30 m) high and up to 2,500 feet (760 m) long. The long, pointed ends of these hills show which way the glacier was moving.

The rocks and sand scooped up and dragged along by glaciers act like sandpaper. They gouged, scratched, and polished the *bedrock* they passed over. In many cases, the scars they left behind filled with glacial meltwaters and became some of our most popular vacation spots— the Great Lakes, the Finger Lakes in New York, and the thousands of small lakes scattered throughout Wisconsin and Minnesota.

As glacial ice grinds its way over the bedrock, it produces a fine material called *rock flour*. When rock flour is carried by a glacier's meltwater into streams and lakes, it turns the water a grayish-blue, and when sunlight bounces off the fine particles, the water looks blue-green. One of the loveliest glacial meltwater lakes in the world is Lake Louise in Banff National Park in Alberta, Canada.

Athabasca Glacier is located at the base of Mount Andromeda in Jasper National Park, Canada. Notice the rock flour in the foreground of this photo.

ANCIENT ICE TELLS TALES

Falling snowflakes stick to volcanic ash, dust particles, tiny drops of acid, and other substances that hang in the air. By the time snow reaches the ground, it is covered with all kinds of materials. If the snow doesn't melt and eventually becomes firn, the materials it picked up from the air become part of the firn, too.

Scientists who study firn often see materials from the atmosphere as well as tiny bits of plants, insects, and bubbles of trapped air. Because the materials in firn are slightly different each year, scientists can use ice *core samples*—long, tubelike pieces of ice removed from a glacier with a special drill—to learn about Earth's history.

In a 100-year-old sample from Alaska or Canada, it is easy to identify the layer of ice from 1912. When a volcano erupted in Alaska that year, the wind carried volcanic ash and dust eastward more than 2,000 miles (3,220 km).

A snowflake on a hemlock branch

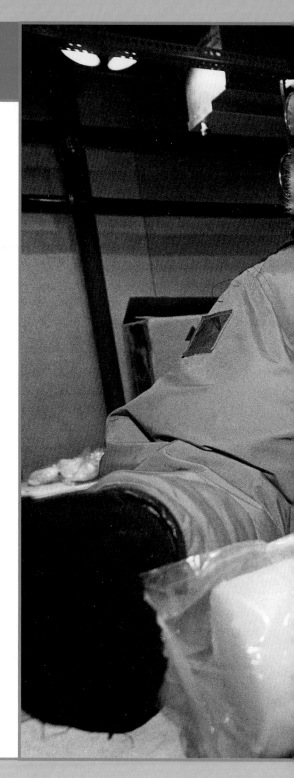

Lonnie Thompson, Ice Scientist

Lonnie Thompson works at the Byrd Polar Research Center at Ohio State University. He has studied ice core samples from glaciers all over the world. He has drilled samples from ice sheets in Greenland and Antarctica and from mountain glaciers in South America, Africa, and China.

In one sample from Greenland, he was able to find out what Earth was like 30,000 years ago. As he studied that sample, he recognized layers deposited between 1961 and 1963 because they contained a material given off by nuclear-bomb tests done during those years. He also identified the layer deposited in 1815. The ice showed signs of a volcanic eruption that had occurred that year in Indonesia.

By studying the air bubbles from the sample, Thompson could tell which years were warmest and which were coldest. And the thickness of the layers told him how much snow had fallen each year.

Glaciologist Lonnie Thompson is removing an ice core sample from a storage area. All of the samples behind him were taken from a single glacier in 1997.

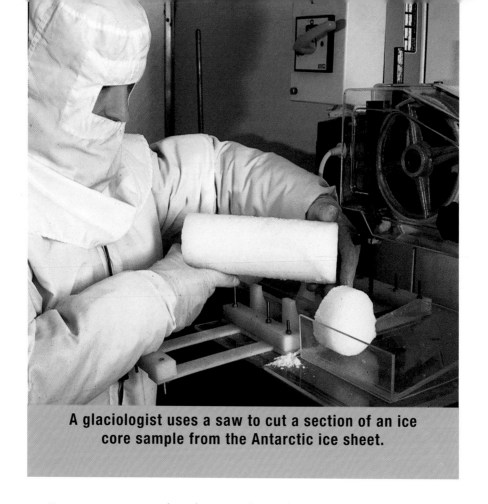

A glaciologist uses a saw to cut a section of an ice core sample from the Antarctic ice sheet.

Ice cores can also be used to determine the age of a glacier. This technique is something like counting a tree's growth rings to figure out how old it is.

Glaciologists are especially interested in the tiny air bubbles found in ice core samples. They can tell us a great deal about the *climate* on Earth in the past. Studying the air helps scientists find out when our planet was moist and when it was dry. The air also lets us know when Earth was warm and when it was cool.

Using recently developed technology, scientists have been able to drill core samples that include layers deposited 160,000 years ago. These Antarctic samples include evidence of the most recent ice age, the interglacial period that came before it, and the ice age before that.

By comparing ice cores from various parts of the world, glaciologists are slowly piecing together information about the climate on Earth thousands of years ago. This work is important to all of us because it may help us understand how human activities can cause climate changes. How do pollution, ozone depletion, and deforestation affect the climate of our world? Studying ancient ice may provide the answers.

Perito Moreno Glacier in Argentina

GLACIERS AROUND THE WORLD

Although massive ice sheets are found only near the North and South Poles, smaller ice sheets are easier to visit, and valley glaciers exist on every continent except Australia.

Some of the most spectacular valley glaciers in the world surround the Gulf of Alaska. In the Southern Hemisphere, some of the most stunning valley glaciers are located in the Andes mountain range between Chile and Argentina.

In Africa, you can find impressive glaciers atop Mount Kenya and Mount Kilimanjaro. Even though these giant mountains are close to the equator, they are icy cold at the top. The Pacific island of New Guinea, which is also close to the equator, has giant glaciers, too. New Zealand also has a wealth of glaciers.

Europe's Caucasus Mountain Range, tucked between the Black Sea and the Caspian Sea, is sprinkled with

Franz Josef Glacier in Westland
National Park, New Zealand

Inspiration Glacier in North Cascades
National Park, Washington

hundreds of glaciers. More than 1,000 glaciers lie along the slopes of the Alps. While some are as small as a football field, others are huge. The Great Aletsch Glacier, for example, is nearly 17 miles (27 km) long. Norway and Sweden have small ice sheets that contain almost as much glacial ice as the Caucasuses and Alps combined.

About 5,000 miles (8,000 km) east of the Alps are the world's highest peaks. These mountains—the Karakoram Range, the Hindu Kush, the Tien Shan, the Kunlun Shan, the Himalaya, and the Pamirs—have many glaciers, too. The Fedtchenko Glacier, located among the Pamirs Range in Asia, is the largest valley glacier in the world. This glacier, which is fed by ice from twenty-five smaller glaciers is nearly 3,000 feet (915 m) thick and 48 miles (77 km) long.

In North America, valley glaciers are found in the Cascade Range and the Coast Mountains, which are located between Alaska and Washington. Smaller glaciers dot the Sierra Nevada mountains and the northern part of the Rocky Mountains.

Visiting Mountain Glaciers

If you would like to find out more about glaciers in North America—or plan a trip to see them—write to the parks listed in this table. You can also contact the Geological Survey Department in your area.

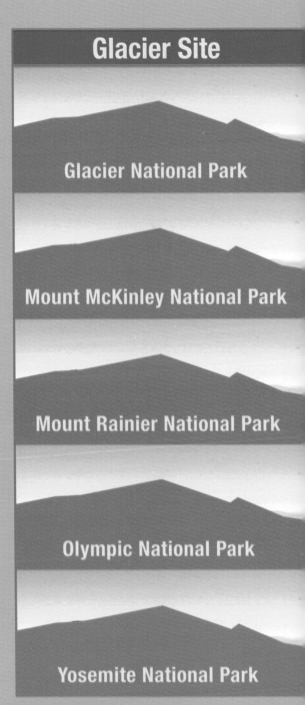

Glacier Site

Glacier National Park

Mount McKinley National Park

Mount Rainier National Park

Olympic National Park

Yosemite National Park

NORTH AMERICA

Features	Contact
The park has 700 miles (1,127 km) of hiking trails and spectacular views.	Park Superintendent Glacier National Park Box 128 West Glacier, MT 59936
Mount McKinley is the highest peak in North America. It is 20,320 feet (6,194 m) tall. The largest glaciers are on the mountain's south side.	Park Superintendent Mount McKinley National Park Box 2252 Anchorage, AK 99051
This park has twenty-eight glaciers and many glacial lakes. Paradise Glacier with its beautiful ice caves is easily accessible. The largest glacier, Emmons Glacier, flows down the northeast flank. Nisqually Glacier has heaps of gravel dumped as a moraine.	Park Superintendent Mount Rainier National Park Longmire, WA 98297
This park has many large "erratic" boulders that were carried down from the mountains of western British Columbia during the last glacial period. At least sixty glaciers, six on Mount Olympus, are still active.	Park Superintendent Olympic National Park 600 East Park Avenue Port Angeles, WA 98362
Many reminders of the last glacial period are found here, including the "hanging" valleys high above the main valley floor and clear mountain lakes fed by glacial meltwater.	Park Superintendent Yosemite National Park Box 577 Yosemite National Park, CA 95389

GLOSSARY

axis—the imaginary line that runs between the North Pole and the South Pole. Earth spins around this line once every 24 hours.

atmosphere—the gases that surround a planet.

bedrock—the solid layer of rock beneath the soil.

calving—the process by which icebergs are created. As a glacier moves off land and over the ocean, large chunks of ice break off along weak points.

core sample—a long cylinder-shaped sample of material. Ice core samples are carefully drilled out of glaciers.

climate—a region's weather averaged over a long time.

crevasse—a deep crack or crevice.

extinct—no longer existing.

firn—snow that has fallen during previous years and been compacted under the weight of new snow.

glacier—a large mass of snow and ice that moves due to its own weight.

gravity—a force that pulls objects toward the center of Earth.

ice age—any extended period of time during which a substantial part of Earth's surface is covered by ice.

ice sheet—a large sheet of ice that flows outward from a central point, such as the Antarctica and Greenland ice sheets.

iceberg—a floating chunk of ice that had broken off a glacier. Only a small part of an iceberg is visible above the surface of the water.

interglacial period—the period of time between two succeeding ice ages. An interglacial period may last for 10,000 years or more.

jökulhlaup—in Iceland, a term for a catastrophic flood the occurs when lava erupts from a volcano and melts huge amounts of glacial ice. The resulting water collects in a gigantic pool. At some stage the water sweeps over the land at about 60 miles (97 km) an hour.

moraine—soil and rocks picked up as a glacier scrapes across the land and then dumped in one spot as the glacier melts.

piedmont glacier—a valley glacier that spreads out when it moves into a large, flat area of land.

rock flour—rock crushed and pulverized by the action of glacial ice and carried by streams into glacial lakes.

valley glacier—a glacier that flows along the floor of a valley.

RESOURCES

Books

Bramwell, Martyn. *Glaciers and Ice Caps*. New York: Franklin Watts, 1994.

Kent, Deborah. *The Titanic*. Chicago: Children's Press, 1993.

Lepthien, Emilie. *Iceland*. Chicago: Children's Press, 1994.

Williams, Jean. *Matthew Henson: Polar Adventurer*. New York: Franklin Watts, 1994.

Web Sites

Glacier has all kinds of information on the formation and movement of glaciers. The site includes many photographs and diagrams. You can also find out how to become a glaciologist. The address is: **http://www.glacier.rice.edu/ chapters/land/5_tableofcontents.html**.

The Glacier Research Group is an organization dedicated to recovering and studying ice core samples. To learn about climate changes throughout Earth's history look at their home page. The address is: **http://breeze.sr.unh.edu/**.

The *Worthington Glacier Project* site describes the work currently being done at the Worthington Glacier in Alaska. This site's address is **http://www.gg.uwyo.edu:8889/**.

Index

ABOUT THE AUTHOR

Roy A. Gallant has been called "one of the deans of American science writers for children" by *School Library Journal*. He has written more than eighty books for children on topics including astronomy, earth science, and evolution. Some recent titles include: *Geysers: When Earth Roars*, *Sand on the Move: The Story of Dunes*, and *Limestone Caves*.

Professor Gallant has worked at the American Museum of Natural History and has been a member of the faculty of New York City's Hayden Planetarium. He is currently the director of the Southworth Planetarium at the University of Southern Maine, where he also holds an adjunct full professorship. He lives in Rangeley, Maine.